Toasty Toes

Counting by Tens

by **Michael Dahl**

illustrated by **Zachary Trover**

Special thanks to our advisers for their expertise:

Stuart Farm, M.Ed., Mathematics Lecturer
University of North Dakota, Grand Forks

Susan Kesselring, M.A., Literacy Educator
Rosemount-Apple Valley-Eagan (Minnesota) School District

PICTURE WINDOW BOOKS
Minneapolis, Minnesota

Editor: Christianne Jones
Designer: Jaime Martens
Page Production: Angela Kilmer
Creative Director: Keith Griffin
Editorial Director: Carol Jones
The illustrations in this book were created digitally.

Picture Window Books
1710 Roe Crest Drive
North Mankato, MN 56003
www.capstonepub.com

Copyright © 2006 by Picture Window Books, a Capstone
imprint. All rights reserved. No part of this book may be
reproduced without written permission from the publisher.
The publisher takes no responsibility for the use of any of
the materials or methods described in this book, nor for
the products thereof.

Library of Congress Cataloging-in-Publication Data
Dahl, Michael.
Toasty toes : counting by tens/ by Michael Dahl ; illustrated
by Zachary Trover.
p. cm. — (Know your numbers)
Includes bibliographical references and index.
ISBN: 978-1-4048-1320-5 (hardcover)
ISBN: 978-1-4048-1926-9 (paperback)
1. Counting—Juvenile literature. 2. Addition—Juvenile
literature. 3. Toes—Juvenile literature. I. Trover, Zachary,
ill. II. Title.

QA113.D3546 2006
513.2'11—dc22   2005021842

The hot morning sun shines on the empty beach.

TEN toes climb up to the lifeguard's stand.

10

TWENTY toes jog through the shallow waves.

20

THIRTY toes race over the warm, toasty sand.

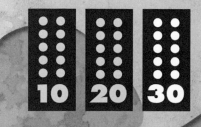

10 20 30 40

FORTY toes walk on the dock.

50

10 20 30 40 50

12

FIFTY toes wiggle in the water.

10 20 30 40 50 60

14

SIXTY toes ride the rushing surf.

15

SEVENTY toes line up
at the ice-cream stand.

10 20 30 40 50 60 70 80

EIGHTY toes jump around the volleyball court.

NINETY toes gather by a sand castle.

10 20 30 40 50 60 70 80 90

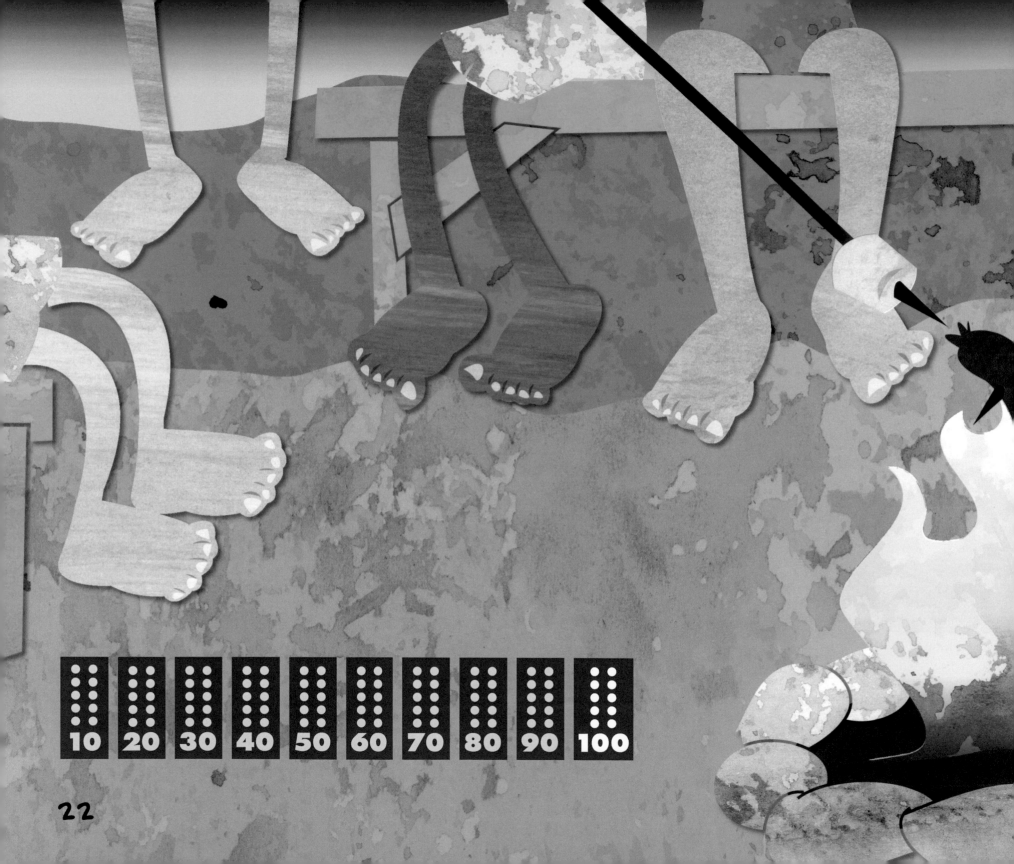

22

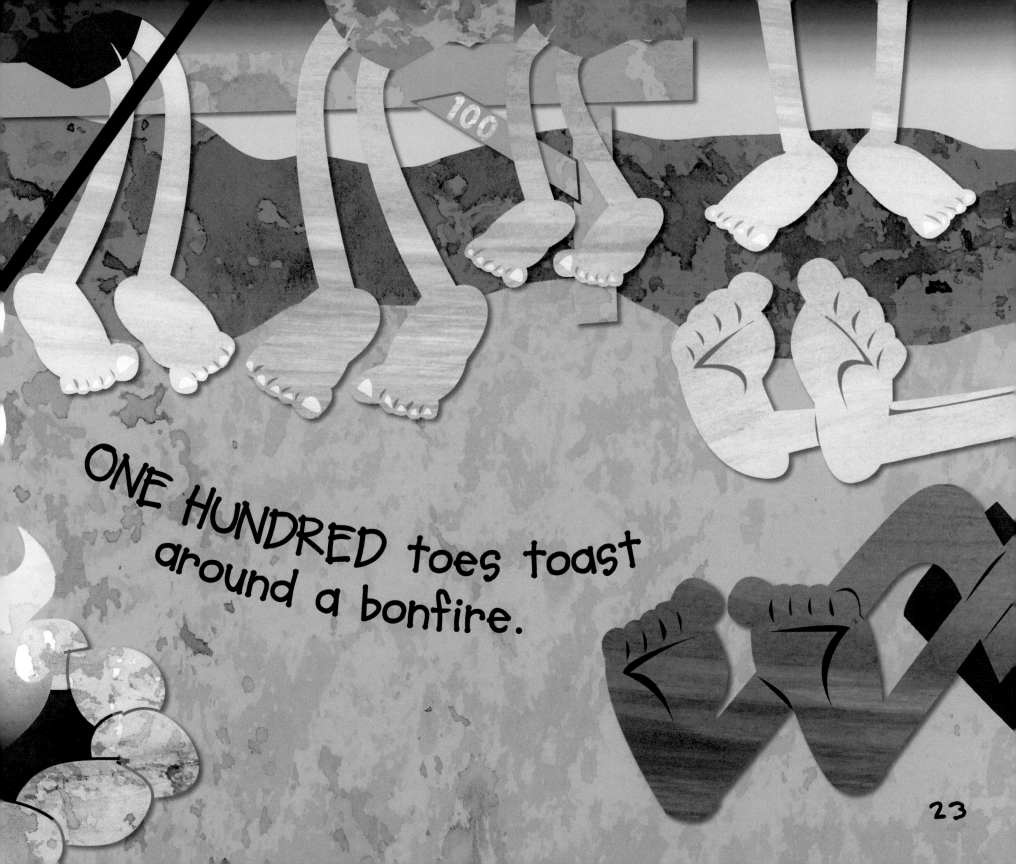

ONE HUNDRED toes toast around a bonfire.

Fun Facts

 The outer layer of skin around your toes absorbs more water than the inner layers. With the extra water inside, the skin expands and wrinkles.

 One fourth of all the bones in your body are in your feet.

 The soles, or bottoms of your feet, have the thickest skin on your body.

 Toe bones are called phalanges. The big toe is called the hallux.

 On beaches, shoes and sandals protect feet from sharp objects that may be hidden in the sand.

On the Web

FactHound offers a safe, fun way to find Internet sites related to this book. All of the sites on FactHound have been researched by our staff.

1. Visit *www.facthound.com*
2. Type in this special code for age-appropriate sites: 1404813209
3. Click on the FETCH IT button.

Your trusty FactHound will fetch the best sites for you!

Find the Numbers

Now you have finished reading the story, but a surprise still awaits you. Hidden in each picture is a multiple of ten from 10 to 100. Can you find them all?

10—on the second step from the top
20—on the far right next to the splashing water
30—the shovel's handle
40—on the fishing pole
50—on the green inner tube
60—on the red shorts
70—on the ice-cream cone
80—in the volleyball net
90—in the girl's pigtail
100—on the bench

Look for all of the books in the Know Your Numbers series:

Ants At the Picnic: Counting by Tens
1-4048-1318-7

Bunches of Buttons: Counting by Tens
1-4048-1315-2

Downhill Fun:
A Counting Book About Winter
1-4048-0579-6

Eggs and Legs: Counting By Twos
1-4048-0945-7

Footprints in the Snow: Counting By Twos
1-4048-0946-5

From the Garden:
A Counting Book About Growing Food
1-4048-0578-8

Hands Down: Counting By Fives
1-4048-0948-1

Lots of Ladybugs! Counting By Fives
1-4048-0944-9

On the Launch Pad:
A Counting Book About Rockets
1-4048-0581-8

One Big Building:
A Counting Book About Construction
1-4048-0580-X

One Checkered Flag:
A Counting Book About Racing
1-4048-0576-1

One Giant Splash:
A Counting Book About the Ocean
1-4048-0577-X

Pie for Piglets: Counting By Twos
1-4048-0943-0

Plenty of Petals: Counting by Tens
1-4048-1317-9

Speed, Speed, Centipede!
Counting by Tens
1-4048-1316-0

Starry Arms: Counting By Fives
1-4048-0947-3

Tail Feather Fun: Counting By Tens
1-4048-1319-5

Toasty Toes: Counting By Tens
1-4048-1320-9